Crumbs
Don't Count

The Rationalization Diet

MARK BINDER

Illustrated by William Bramhall

Animation by
J.J. Sedelmaier Productions, Inc.
Mike Wetterhahn, Animator

AVON BOOKS ◆ **NEW YORK**

AVON BOOKS, INC.
1350 Avenue of the Americas
New York, New York 10019

Copyright © 1998 by Mark Binder
Interior illustrations © 1998 by Avon Books
Illustrated by William Bramhall. Animation by J.J. Sedelmaier
Productions, Inc. Mike Wetterhahn, Animator.
Front cover illustration by William Bramhall
Published by arrangement with the author
Visit our website at **http://www.AvonBooks.com**
Library of Congress Catalog Card Number: 98-92810
ISBN: 0-380-80015-2

First Avon Books Trade Printing: July 1998

AVON TRADEMARK REG. U.S. PAT. OFF. AND IN OTHER COUNTRIES, MARCA
REGISTRADA, HECHO EN U.S.A.

Printed in the U.S.A.

QPM 10 9 8 7 6 5 4 3 2 1

Acknowledgments

Thanks to: Alicia Lehrer, David Adler, Eve Bladstrom, Dara Chadwick, Mom and Dad, Andrea and Jonathan, Chris Golden, Pam Liflander, Nora Forbes, Matty and Jean Forbes, Kim and John Worthington, Gen Germann, The Taste Society, Serena Camacho, Emily Kirts, Mrs. Adler and Equitable Travel, Kevin Mallon, FileMaker Pro, Barden Prisant, Whitman Field, Linda Asta, Debbie Hawkins, Rob and Mark at Solvent Media . . .

and especially
Holley Bishop and Charlotte Abbott

It has sometimes seemed to me . . . that to the modern craze for dieting may be attributed all the unhappiness which is afflicting the world today.

—P.G. WODEHOUSE,
THE WORLD OF MR. MULLINER

Contents

Introduction

All the rationalizations in *Crumbs Don't Count* are "true." They may not be logical, scientific, or even accurate—but common sense, intuition, and creativity tell us that these previously unspoken rules and suggestions are in fact "true."

You will, no doubt, realize that there are many, many more rationalizations and variations on the themes. In fact, there is a rationalization for every food-related dilemma.

Thin people may not understand: There is a cruel line that stands between you and that chocolate chip cookie.

Crumbs Don't Count crosses that line.

Remember: Any excuse to eat is a good excuse.

THE BASICS

Hors d'oeuvres don't count . . . as long as you're having dinner later.

(Also, food eaten with your fingers has fewer calories than food eaten with a knife and fork.)

Dressing on the side has no calories and less fat, especially if you only dip things into it.

''Just a little taste''
doesn't count.

If no one sees you eat it,
it has no calories.

Smaller plates hold fewer calories.

•

Two small pieces have fewer
calories than one big one.

•

One more bite really doesn't
matter.

Crumbs don't count.

Definition of a Crumb

Any part of a whole that is less than one-eighth the size of the whole itself.

<u>The One-Inch Exception</u>: If the whole is smaller than one inch in diameter, a crumb is less than one-quarter the size of the whole.

<u>The Doughnut Standard</u>*: A crumb is smaller than one-eighth of a doughnut; there are at least 9 crumbs to a doughnut.

---

*We have chosen the doughnut as a measurement standard because it is universal within the United States, and tasty. Don't worry about the doughnut's size, however; that's not the point. Try to find fresh ones. They taste better.

A Crumbly Recipe

Ingredients
1 to 1½ lb. Oreo cookies
  (still in package)
Hammer
8 oz. milk (optional)

1. Place bag or box of Oreos on a firm surface; a table, chopping block, or the floor will do quite well.
2. Apply blunt end of hammer to the box. Do this with joy and abandon. Take out all your frustrations. Be creative. Continue until Oreos are crushed.
3. Pour crumbs into a bowl.
4. Add optional milk and eat with a spoon.

Substitutions: Chips Ahoy, Nilla Wafers, etc.

If it's not listed in the calorie book,
it has no calories.

If it smells good,
you must eat some.

RESTAURANT RATIONALIZATIONS:

Dining Out Without Guilt

If you share your meal, the other person gets all the calories.

Calories are attributed to the person who ordered the dish.

A salad without dressing
neutralizes
the fat content
of fettucini Alfredo.

When you give someone a taste
from your dish,
they get half the calories for
the entire dish.

In other words,
If two people taste your dish,
there are no calories left.

•

If three or more people try your
dish, you actually lose weight!

Steal it off of another person's
plate, and they get the calories.

Salad that comes with dinner has no calories.

(Actually, anything you didn't order that comes with the dinner has no calories.

This includes bread, bread sticks, and after-dinner mints.)

Appetizers don't count,

and

house specialties *never* count.

You're legally entitled to dessert
if you

take the skin off the chicken, and
eat the baked potato with lemon
juice instead of sour cream and
butter.

Anything à la carte has fewer calories than the same dish as an entrée.

New restaurants don't count . . .
They're research.

•

If the restaurant owner comes to
your table, you must clean your
plate or else she'll be offended.

•

When the waiter removes the
plates before you're done, all
calories are reduced by 5 percent.

Whoever eats the last bite
gets all the calories.

DESSERTS YOU
DESERVE

Eating dessert before dinner is OK
because you won't eat as much at
dinner.

Cookie Chicanery

M&M cookies are simply a vehicle for M&Ms; the cookie doesn't count.

•

Two (or more) cookies stuck together only count as one.

•

If you don't throw out the box, the last cookie doesn't count.

Nutritionists recommend at least
1,200 calories a day—might as
well make some of it candy.

The size of the dessert *must* be proportional to the rottenness of the day you've had.

After all, you've already burned off plenty of calories in anxiety and frustration.

Frosting on the cake plate
has no calories.

A fingerful of frosting is
both negligible and necessary . . .

Since no one will notice it's
missing, it isn't.

Also, if you don't taste the cake,
how will you know it isn't
poisoned?

Frozen candy bars have fewer
calories than candy bars at room
temperature.

Melted ice cream has fewer
calories than frozen ice cream.

(The calories have evaporated!)

Half a slice of pie (or cake) has
one-quarter the calories of a
whole slice.

•

Slivers have no calories.

If you drink a diet soda while eating a hot fudge sundae, the soda cancels out the sundae.

•

Cake and ice cream have about the same calories; therefore, putting a scoop of ice cream on cake adds no calories.

Shared desserts have *no* calories.

Waste Reduction

Once you take a bite of something, especially chocolate, you must finish it, because otherwise it would be wasteful.

The exception is an entire box of chocolates, where sample bites of every piece don't count—it's a scientific experiment to determine which tastes best and which has the caramel center.

Twinkies have a twenty-year
shelf-life, therefore,

they count as a preservative rather
than as a dessert.

You can cancel out cake by eating carrots.

•

Jell-O isn't fattening.

•

If you refuse any dessert three times, it loses one-third of its fat.

You must finish a meal with
dessert so your body will know
you're done eating.

EXCUSES FOR THE
HOME

Homemade cookies have fewer
calories than store-bought.

Food tasted while you are cooking
has absolutely no calories.

•

Food eaten while cleaning up is
considered recycling.

Batter licked from the cookie bowl
isn't eating, it's verifying the
recipe.

Breakfast has fewer calories than lunch, which has fewer calories than dinner.

(Note: any food eaten before noon is considered breakfast.)

However,
Eating breakfast for dinner is less fattening than eating breakfast for breakfast or dinner for dinner.

Rice Krispie Treats aren't dessert,
they're breakfast.

The Spoilage Factor

You *must* eat anything that will spoil while you defrost your freezer or if your power goes out . . .

. . . especially ice cream.

New recipes have no calories.

If someone else does the dishes,
they get the calories.

•

If you get stuck doing the dishes,
not only do *they* get the calories
but you actually burn calories
from the exercise.

Meat cooked at a low temperature
has less fat.

(Really!)

Mom's Favorite

Leave some on your plate and the calories you've eaten will be reduced by the value of the remnants.

Leftovers have fewer calories
than the meal itself.

•

Leftovers eaten with a small
utensil (like a tea spoon or dessert
fork) have even fewer calories.

ALIBIS FOR THE OFFICE

Take-out Chinese food has no
calories if you work through
lunch.

Breakfast in the car has fewer calories than the same meal at home.

•

Anything ordered from a drive-up window has fewer calories than the same thing ordered standing in line.

Morning doughnuts are burned off
in the anxiety and boredom of
staff meetings.

Office Parties

When you organize an office party, everyone else gets all the calories.

•

When someone throws an office party for you, you're exempt as guest of honor.

The irresistible smell of
microwaving popcorn
distributes the calories evenly
throughout the entire office.

Eating at your desk
isn't really a meal.

Coffee with cream and sugar
is part of your job description.

Food Loses Calories Over Time

A Snickers bar stored for a month
in a desk drawer has fewer
calories than correction fluid.

Food consumed on a deadline is
reduced by the factor of urgency.

Girl Scout Cookies

The guy selling his daughter's Girl Scout cookies gets all the calories for all the boxes sold at the office.

However, if you sell Girl Scout cookies for your daughter, then your co-workers get all the calories for cookies you eat at home!

Finally, it doesn't really matter—all calories from Girl Scout cookies go to a good cause.

A business lunch is a business
expense—the calories are
deductible.

ON THE ROAD:

Rationalizations for Travel

and Vacation

Travel "Exercise"

1. You burn off one dessert if you look up the hotel gym's phone number and learn its hours.

2. Watching limbo or chicken dancers counts as a workout.

The Language–Fat Barrier

Both fat and calories are lost
across the language barrier.

•

In other words, if you don't
understand the language, how can
you possibly absorb the food.
Examples include:
fromage
hollandaise
à la mode
au gratin,
huevos
cerveza
pommes fritte

Rum drinks purchased in the
Caribbean are duty free, and
therefore calorie free.

Food delivered by room service
has fewer calories than the same
meals eaten in the hotel
restaurant.

The Foul-Weather Diet

If it rains or is cloudy while you're
taking a beach vacation, the foul
weather gets all the calories.

The Patriotism Rationalization

If you're in France and don't speak French, it's up to you to order the most fattening and expensive dish on the menu to prove you know what French food's all about.

Food purchased at open air
markets has no calories.

(Especially if it gives you the runs.)

If an alarm clock goes off
while you're on vacation,
breakfast is void.

Mosquitoes eat the calories, too.

The "Native Food" Exemptions

1. Local custom, the locals get the calories.
2. Local holiday, the locals get the calories.
3. Strange wrappings or breads absorb most of the calories. This includes: banana leaves, tobacco leaves, bowls made out of coconuts or fried tortillas, fufu, naan, and newspaper-wrapped fish and chips.
4. Anything eaten from a basket has fewer calories than the same food from a plate.
5. Fried food on vacation has fewer calories than broiled food at home.

On family vacations, the rest of
the family gets the calories.

WEDDINGS,
BAR MITZVAHS,
DINNER PARTIES,
DATES, AND
FUNERALS . . .

Food from a buffet has fewer
calories than the same dish eaten
at a sit-down meal.

The Politeness Effect

If someone gives you chocolate, you must eat it because it's polite*

*The Japanese have known the importance of politeness in diet for centuries. Did you know that every bow burns between one and two calories, depending on its deepness? Thus by being incredibly polite, the Japanese have found a simple and effective way to maintain their slenderness. While handshaking is not as effective a form of exercise as bowing (a truly vigorous handshake only burns about one-quarter of a calorie) a polite dieter can add a variety of extra actions to increase the Politeness Effect. For instance, a slap on the back (.1 calorie), a hug (.25 to 3 calories), kiss on the cheek (.1 calorie), kiss on the lips (.2 to 10 calories), and so on. As you see, the more polite you are, the more weight you'll lose, and the more you'll be able to eat. Thus politeness breeds thinness and happiness, something the Japanese know intimately.

The exceptions, of course, are sumo wrestlers, who are very polite. Because they are so fat, they can't bow deeply. They do, however, enjoy their food anyway.

The stress of a first date creates an energy imbalance, sucking extra calories out of your food.

Four Principles of Social Functions

1. Food eaten at benefits is a contribution to the cause.
2. Calories consumed at family occasions are burned off in anxiety.
3. When you're a guest, it is impolite to leave the last piece because it might offend your host, so all calories are deferred to Emily Post.
4. When you're the host, it's impolite to make your guest feel like a pig, so you must eat the last piece.

At Weddings and Bar Mitzvahs

If you try *all* the hors d'oeuvres,
you get no calories during dinner!

More Principles of Social Functions

1. It's rude to refuse a second helping. You don't want to offend your host.
2. It's also impolite to leave food on your plate.
3. If you're visiting for a long weekend, it's impolite to leave food in the host's refrigerator.

It's OK to eat if everybody else is eating.

Of course, if nobody else is eating, somebody has to start or we'll all starve!

If it's broken, it's guilt free
because it's imperfect and you
can't serve that to company.

Movie Rules

1. After the lights go down, no calories count.
2. Popcorn is included in the price of admission.
3. If you've already seen the movie, and you're watching it again on video, the microwave popcorn doesn't count. (Intending to see the movie in the theater is equivalent to actually seeing it.)
4. Nothing mixed in with the popcorn (M&Ms, Starburst, nonpareils) counts.

More Movie Rules

5. Popcorn is a vegetable.

6. Butter on popcorn is fattening, but chances are whatever you're getting on your popcorn isn't really butter anyway, so don't worry about it.

7. Anything you sneak into the theater is fat-free.

8. If you get ejected from the theater for sneaking things in, the usher gets the calories.

9. Twizzlers and Starburst—no matter what the ingredients say—are made out of plastic and have no nutritive value, calories, or fat whatsoever.

The Movie Make-Out Isometric Exercise (for guys only)

Having your arm around the shoulder for your date for the bulk of the movie certainly counts as exercise.

After all, your arm's stiff, so you've obviously been doing a good deal of work with it.

HOLIDAYS:

The Rationalizer's Calendar

Nothing Counts on Your Birthday

Other celebrations at which you are entitled to eat as much as you want:

- First day on new job
- Last day on new job
- Retirement day
- Your wedding day
- Divorce finalized

Seasonal Rationalizations

First day of spring: "This is the last day I can eat if I want to fit into my summer bathing suit."

First day of summer: "Can't fit into my summer bathing suit today, so I might as well have an ice cream."

First day of autumn: "I just burned the bathing suit. Let's get sundaes!"

First day of winter: "It's getting cold. I'd better build up a layer of fat."

Super Bowl Sunday

1. Reaching for the chips is considered exercise.

2. Beer has no calories.

On Valentine's Day . . .

- If your lover gives you candy, you must eat it.
- If no one gives you candy, you must get some and eat it.
- Chocolate syrup licked off someone else's body has no calories.*

*Actually, this is true on any day.

On St. Patrick's Day:

Drinking beer is a form of worship.

During Passover...

- Matzoh has no calories.
- Anything made with matzoh has no calories.
- You have to eat all those eggs because the matzoh tastes so bland.
- Besides, God commanded you to change your diet, so *nothing* counts.

Easter Time

During Lent, fried fish has
no calories on Fridays.

•

On Easter, ham, chocolate,
marshmallow bunnies and lambs,
Easter eggs, and jelly beans are
transubstantiated into symbols.

Symbols have no fat or calories.

Halloween

You must taste all your child's candy to make sure it's not poisoned.

Thanksgiving

Thanksgiving is a lost cause.

It's a national holiday
based around feasting.

Whoever eats the most, wins.

The Twelve Rationalizations of Christmas

1. After Thanksgiving, nothing's going to matter anyway.
2. Holidays depress me. Food makes me happy!
3. Family's coming.
4. Family's here.
5. We only have goose once a year.
6. I won't eat the fruitcake.
7. But I cooked it . . .
8. But Grandma cooked it . . .
9. Christmas cookies are part of the meal.
10. *Someone* has to eat Santa's cookies.
11. I can always return the gifts that don't fit . . .
12. I'll make a New Year's resolution.

On New Year's Eve...

- Alcohol has no calories—if you're on a blind date, alone, at an office party, in a bar wearing a pointy hat, single, or married.
- You can eat anything and everything you want because you're just going to make a New Year's resolution about it anyway.
- The hammering effect of blood through the brain the next morning will crush any extra calories that might have slipped through.

CREATIVE
RATIONALIZATIONS

Anti-Thin Rationalizations
(What's so great about being thin?)

- Thin people die young.
- Those models in *Vogue* and *Cosmo* are going to get old and fat anyway.
- Thin people die of hypothermia faster, so if you're on a cruise in the Arctic or Antarctic, it's better to have a layer of fat.
- Satan is thin.
- Which would you rather sleep on, a bag of bones or a soft downy pillow?
- Thin people have a greater chance of falling through the gratings over sidewalks and sewers.

The JennyCraigDietCenterNutri/ System Diet

You can eat anything we sell you.

The Zone Rationalization

Eat high protein foods for one week. Eat anything you want the next week . . .

or vice versa.

The Pritikin Diet Rationalization

No refined sugar, meat, eggs, fat, alcohol, caffeine, or nicotine . . .

but eat as much pasta and bread as you want.

The Scarsdale Diet Radical Weight-Loss Program

Breakfast: One half grapefruit, one slice of protein toast
Lunch: Murder your lover
Dinner: Whatever they serve at the local lockup
Exercise: Plenty of time for that in prison

Speedy Rationalizations

The faster you eat, the fewer calories are absorbed.

•

If you eat slower, you'll eat less.

•

Food is energy. Sugar gets converted fastest. If you need to move quickly, you'd better eat something with sugar now.

The World's Heaviest Man

The world's heaviest man weighed
1,069 pounds and was buried in a
box the size of a grand piano.
You're *skinny*.

A Dubious Rationalization
(but worth a try)

If you eat under the table, it's
impossible to overeat.

Anything used to cleanse the
palate has no calories,
including (but not limited to):

- Vanilla ice cream
- Sherbet
- Wine
- Beer

Calorie Credits

Anything you give up, you get a
calorie credit for.

When you pass up a 750-calorie
piece of chocolate cake, you get a
body calorie credit. Save it. Use it
later. Invest it. How about mutual
funds?

The Rosie O'Donnell
Drake's Cakes Deduction

You can eat as many
Ding Dongs as you want
—if you're a talk show host.

(or a guest, or in the audience,
or an at-home viewer)

EXERCISE AND OTHER MEDICAL EXCUSES

Doctors say, "The more you exercise, the more you can eat."

Therefore, if you exercise* at all, you can eat more!

Note: If you're the kind of person who doesn't exercise, don't worry, doctors aren't always right.

Three Mental Exercises

1. Thinking about exercising burns one-tenth the calories of actually exercising.
2. Feeling guilty about *not* exercising burns one-fifth the calories.
3. Worrying about whether or not you should eat something is also exercise.

Note: A good workout can include short sprints of worry, followed by marathons of guilt.

A half-hour of exercise
counteracts one full meal
(regardless of the type of exercise
or the size of the meal).

The Exercise Wear Workout

Squeezing into:
sweat sox, sweat pants, a sweat
shirt and a sweat band is exercise
enough.

Have a cookie.

If you drink eight glasses of water
a day, you are allowed to eat
whatever you want.

Female Rationalizations

Menstruation is a valid excuse for eating anything and everything.

•

Any and all weight gained during your period is due to water retention.

•

Pregnant and breast-feeding women are entitled to eat as much as they want.

•

You have to eat *something* with calcium pills, or Motrin.

(Speaking of calcium, doesn't a milkshake have calcium?)

Feed a cold.
Feed a fever.
Feed a hangover.

Eating in Motion

Anything you eat while walking is immediately burned off as energy.

•

Food eaten in a moving car has half the calories.

Hospital Food

Hospital food is inedible.
However, you must eat to get well.
Therefore, anything you sneak into
the hospital is actually medicine.

Calories burned per ten minutes (Depending on metabolism and intensity)

Sitting and watching TV: 8–14
Talking: 12–21
Typing (40 wpm):   15–27
Ping Pong: 26–45
Reading: 30–50

Note: If you read this book very, very, very slowly, you'll work off a doughnut.

Sex and Weight Loss

Anything consumed while trying
to seduce someone is immediately
burned off—whether or not you
get lucky.

•

If you have sex in the morning, no
calories count for the rest of the
day.

•

Really good sex entitles you to eat
chocolates in bed afterward.

ADVANCED
RATIONALIZATIONS

Cold pizza has fewer calories
than warm pizza.

You can eat anything you want when

- You're depressed
- You have diarrhea
- You've been diagnosed with terminal cancer
- Your husband runs away with a gay doctor
- You're in a coma
- All of the above

Small bites have fewer calories
than large bites, therefore, if you
only eat small bites . . .

Containing Calories

Eating from the container has fewer calories than eating from the plate.

This includes eating directly from: ice cream or Chinese food cartons; potato chip bags (works for any chip); pizza boxes; and microwaved popcorn bags.

Not to mention American Cheese food from the wrapper, or Chef Boyardee from the can.

Note: Eat standing up and over the sink for bonus exercise weight loss.

Read Those Labels

You burn 10 calories and 1 gram
of fat every time you read a food
nutrition label.

The Fatalist's Rationalization

Life is short.
If it tastes good, it must be eaten.

If you skip breakfast and lunch,
you can have as much of anything
you want for dinner.

According to Doctors

Children of obese parents have a greater likelihood of becoming overweight.

So, if you're overweight and your parents are overweight, chances are it's their fault.

Therefore, 25 percent of all food consumed is Mom's fault and 25 percent is Dad's.

Plus, if you eat more, it'll just make them fatter.

If you eat like a pig one day, and eat a normal amount or fewer calories the next day, the pig-out day doesn't count.

The Country Music Rationalization

You can drink as much beer as you want when:

Your wife leaves you
Your dog dies
Your truck is stolen

The Two-Word Rationalization

Why not?

"HEALTH FOOD"

Health food doesn't count.

It has no calories.

Anything cooked on a grill has no extra fat, so it makes you thin and healthy.

Fat-free food has no calories.

•

If you think it's not fattening, it
probably isn't, so you might as
well have it.

Salad has no calories

This includes:
antipasto,
tuna salad,
chicken salad,
three-bean salad, or
pasta salad

Celery is a form of exercise.

Fruits and Vegetables

Fruits and vegetables *never* count.

•

Strawberry daiquiris are a fruit.

•

Pesto is a vegetable.

•

Anything green is a vegetable
(except meat).

Any meal in which you eat a lot of vegetables doesn't count.

Caffeine Rationalizations

If you drink a lot of coffee, you burn off extra calories because you'll do everything a little faster and you won't sleep as much.

•

Mountain Dew, which has a very high level of caffeine, is actually a diet aid.

Guar Gum

No one really knows what it is, but guar gum probably destroys calories.

Fast Food

Fast food is good for you.

How?

Because the time you saved
cooking and cleaning can be used
to work out.

(Oh, yeah, right.)

Well, you could . . .

Packaging Rationalizations

- Anything that comes in a green box is a healthy choice.
- Anything lite is nutritious.
- Candy enriched with vitamins doesn't count.
- High protein foods have no calories.
- Anything made with saccharin or NutraSweet is *not* fattening.

Fry It

Vegetable oil is a vegetable.

Vegetables are better for you than meat.

Therefore, anything you eat cooked in vegetable oil is better than the same thing cooked in lard.

Juice is better for you than soda.
Coke is made from cola juice.
(OK, that's a stretch.)

•

Cherry Coke, on the other hand, is
definitely a fruit.

Grapefruit Effects

Eating grapefruit will reduce your weight.

•

Grapefruits burn off fat.

•

The taste of a grapefruit so greatly diminishes your appetite that you lose weight just by smelling one.

The Juicer Diet

Anything you run through a juicer
has fewer calories, no fat, and
must be good for you.

The Fiber Diet

If you eat enough fiber,
nothing else is going to stick.

If buttermilk is good for you,
then both butter and milk
must be good for you.

You can drink as much lite beer as you want without getting fat or drunk.

THE SCIENCE OF RATIONALIZATION:

Theories and Scientific Proof

That Crumbs Don't Count

The Geological Epoch Rationalization

A million years from now none of this matters, so . . . why not eat chocolate?

The Subatomic Corollary

All matter is made of atoms.
Atoms are mostly space.
Space has no calories.
Therefore, a chocolate cake,
which is mostly space,
has no calories.

The Principle of Acidic Reduction

The spicier the food, the fewer the calories.

The Principle of Natural Food

Anything that's less refined is
better.

The Principle of Human Ingenuity

Anything that takes hours of
preparation by a qualified chef (or
chemist) has fewer calories
because energy is lost during the
cooking process.

The Principle of Serving Style

The method of presentation
affects the caloric value of food

(e.g., Pizza in a box has fewer
calories than pizza on a plate).

The Principle of Scientific Revisionism

All scientific studies are dubious.

Whatever they say is bad for you probably isn't, because someone else is doing a study that proves the exact opposite.

(Examples include: Oat bran, butter, beef, eggs, coffee . . .)

The Three Principles of Texture

1. Liquids have fewer calories than solids.
2. Crunchy food is better exercise than soft food.
3. Completely mushy food has no substance, and therefore no calories.

The Reverse Einstein Rationalization

The faster you eat something,
the fewer calories it has.
Thus fewer calories
are actually consumed.

The Principles of Spoilage

1. If it is on someone else's plate, and they are not going to eat it, you may eat it without absorbing a single calorie.
2. If it was going to be thrown out anyway, it has no calories.

The Blown-Diet Principle

Once you've blown your diet
—no matter how minimally—
nothing you eat for the rest of the
day counts, so you might as well
keep on eating.

The Principle of Approaching Infinity

Small enough bites are negligible, therefore, you can eat an infinite amount of small bites without absorbing a single calorie.

The Hell Principle

If you're already way too full,
nothing you eat afterward
has any calories.

The Expanding Universe Theory

The universe is expanding,
why shouldn't your waistline?

The Ultimate Rationalization

Nothing you eat today counts—if you are going to start a diet tomorrow.

•

To contribute your own favorite rationalizations, or to learn about new breakthroughs in the "science" of Crumbs Don't Count . . .

•

Visit our web site at http://www.markbinder.com